Big Rigs
on the Go

by Anne J. Spaight

BUMBA BOOKS™

LERNER PUBLICATIONS ◆ MINNEAPOLIS

Note to Educators:

Throughout this book, you'll find critical thinking questions. These can be used to engage young readers in thinking critically about the topic and in using the text and photos to do so.

Lerner Publications Company
A division of Lerner Publishing Group, Inc.
241 First Avenue North
Minneapolis, MN 55401 USA

For reading levels and more information, look up this title at www.lernerbooks.com.

Library of Congress Cataloging-in-Publication Data

The Cataloging-in-Publication Data for *Big Rigs on the* Go is on file at the Library of Congress.
ISBN 978-1-5124-1450-9 (lib. bdg.)
ISBN 978-1-5124-1491-2 (pbk.)
ISBN 978-1-5124-1492-9 (EB pdf)

Manufactured in the United States of America
1 – VP – 7/15/16

LERNER
SOURCE

Expand learning beyond the printed book. Download free, complementary educational resources for this book from our website, www.lernerresource.com.

Table of Contents

Big Rigs

A big rig is a big truck.

It carries goods across

the country.

A big rig is called a semitruck.

It has a tractor and a trailer.

tractor

trailer

7

The tractor is at the front.

It has the engine.

It has the cab.

The driver sits in the cab.

The trailer is at the back.

It connects to the tractor.

It holds the goods.

What kinds of goods might a trailer hold?

A big rig has eighteen wheels.

The tractor has ten wheels.

The trailer has eight wheels.

A big rig is as heavy as

seven elephants.

It is as long as two

school buses.

Drivers need a special license.

Many go to truck driving school.

Why do you think drivers go to truck driving school?

Some drivers stay close to home.

Others spend weeks on the road.

They have larger cabs with beds.

Why might some cabs have beds?

Big rigs go everywhere.
They deliver most goods
in the United States.

Parts of a Big Rig

tractor

cab

trailer

fuel tank

wheels

22

Picture Glossary

cab

the part of a big rig where the driver sits

goods

things people buy from stores

tractor

the front part of a big rig

trailer

the back part of a big rig

Index

Read More

Carr, Aaron. *Semi Trucks.* New York: AV2 by Weigl, 2016.

Ransom, Candice. *Big Rigs on the Move.* Minneapolis: Lerner Publications, 2011.

Silverman, Buffy. *How Do Big Rigs Work?* Minneapolis: Lerner Publications, 2015.

Photo Credits